People in My Community/La gente de mi comunidad

Bus Driver/
El conductor del autobús

Jacqueline Laks Gorman
photographs by/fotografías de Gregg Andersen

Reading consultant/Consultora de lectura: Susan Nations, M.Ed., author/literacy coach/consultant

WEEKLY WR READER®
EARLY LEARNING LIBRARY

Please visit our web site at: www.garethstevens.com
For a free color catalog describing Weekly Reader® Early Learning Library's
list of high-quality books, call 1-877-445-5824 (USA) or 1-800-387-3178 (Canada).
Weekly Reader® Early Learning Library's fax: (414) 336-0164.

Library of Congress Cataloging-in-Publication Data

Gorman, Jacqueline Laks, 1955-
    [Bus driver. Spanish & English]
    Bus driver = El conductor del autobús / by Jacqueline Laks Gorman.
       p. cm. — (People in my community = La gente de mi comunidad)
    Summary: Introduces the work of the bus driver, who helps people by
taking them where they want to go.
    Includes bibliographical references and index.
    ISBN 0-8368-3306-6 (lib. bdg.)
    ISBN 0-8368-3340-6 (softcover)
    1. Bus driving—Juvenile literature. 2. Bus drivers—Juvenile literature.
[1. Bus drivers. 2. Buses. 3. Occupations. 4. Spanish language
materials—Bilingual.] I. Title: Conductor del autobús. II. Title.
    TL232.3.G6718   2002
    388.3'22044'092—dc21
                               2002066387

Updated and reprinted in 2006
This edition first published in 2002 by
Weekly Reader® Early Learning Library
A Member of the WRC Media Family of Companies
330 West Olive Street, Suite 100
Milwaukee, WI 53212 USA

Copyright © 2002 by Weekly Reader® Early Learning Library

Art direction and page layout: Tammy West
Photographer: Gregg Andersen
Editorial assistant: Diane Laska-Swanke
Production: Susan Ashley
Translators: Tatiana Acosta and Guillermo Gutiérrez

Printed in the United States of America

8 9 10 09 08 07 06

Note to Educators and Parents

Reading is such an exciting adventure for young children! They are beginning to integrate their oral language skills with written language. To encourage children along the path to early literacy, books must be colorful, engaging, and interesting; they should invite the young reader to explore both the print and the pictures.

People in My Community is a new series designed to help children read about the world around them. In each book young readers will learn interesting facts about some familiar community helpers.

Each book is specially designed to support the young reader in the reading process. The familiar topics are appealing to young children and invite them to read — and re-read — again and again. The full-color photographs and enhanced text further support the student during the reading process.

In addition to serving as wonderful picture books in schools, libraries, homes, and other places where children learn to love reading, these books are specifically intended to be read within an instructional guided reading group. This small group setting allows beginning readers to work with a fluent adult model as they make meaning from the text. After children develop fluency with the text and content, the book can be read independently. Children and adults alike will find these books supportive, engaging, and fun!

Una nota a los educadores y a los padres

¡La lectura es una emocionante aventura para los niños! En esta etapa están comenzando a integrar su manejo del lenguaje oral con el lenguaje escrito. Para fomentar la lectura desde una temprana edad, los libros deben ser vistosos, atractivos e interesantes; deben invitar al joven lector a explorar tanto el texto como las ilustraciones.

La gente de mi comunidad es una nueva serie pensada para ayudar a los niños a conocer el mundo que los rodea. En cada libro, los jóvenes lectores conocerán datos interesantes sobre el trabajo de distintas personas de la comunidad.

Cada libro ha sido especialmente diseñado para facilitar el proceso de lectura. La familiaridad con los temas tratados atrae la atención de los niños y los invita a leer — y releer — una y otra vez. Las fotografías a todo color y el tipo de letra facilitan aún más al estudiante el proceso de lectura.

Además de servir como fantásticos libros ilustrados en la escuela, la biblioteca, el hogar y otros lugares donde los niños aprenden a amar la lectura, estos libros han sido concebidos específicamente para ser leídos en grupos de instrucción guiada. Este contexto de grupos pequeños permite que los niños que se inician en la lectura trabajen con un adulto cuya fluidez les sirve de modelo para comprender el texto. Una vez que se han familiarizado con el texto y el contenido, los niños pueden leer los libros por su cuenta. ¡Tanto niños como adultos encontrarán que estos libros son útiles, entretenidos y divertidos!

— Susan Nations, M.Ed., author, literacy coach,
and consultant in literacy development

The bus driver has an important job. The bus driver helps people.

— — — — — — —

El trabajo del conductor del autobús es muy importante. El conductor ayuda a la gente.

The bus driver helps
people by taking them
where they want to go.

— — — — — — — —

El conductor del autobús
ayuda a la gente
llevándola a donde
quiere ir.

Bus drivers have to be safe drivers. They have to follow all the driving rules.

- - - - - - - -

Los conductores de autobús tienen que manejar con cuidado. Deben respetar todas las normas.

The bus driver goes
along the same streets
and stops at the same
places every day.

El conductor del autobús
pasa por las mismas
calles y hace las
mismas paradas todos
los días.

When the bus driver
stops the bus,
passengers get
on and off the bus.

- - - - - - - -

Cuando el conductor
para el autobús,
los pasajeros bajan
y suben.

When passengers get on the bus, they give the bus driver a fare.

Cuando los pasajeros suben al autobús, le pagan el billete al conductor.

The school bus driver
is a special type of bus
driver. He takes children
to and from school.

- - - - - - - -

El conductor del
autobús escolar lleva
a los niños a la escuela
y a sus casas.

You have to listen to the school bus driver. You have to behave on the school bus.

Cuando estás en el autobús escolar, debes hacerle caso al conductor. Debes portarte bien.

It looks like fun to be a bus driver. Would you like to be a bus driver some day?

Ser conductor de autobús parece divertido. ¿Te gustaría ser conductor de autobús algún día?

Glossary/Glosario

behave — to act in a good way

portarse bien — actuar como se debe

fare — what you pay to ride on a bus or train

billete — lo que se compra para subir a un autobús o a un tren

passengers — the people who ride with the driver on a bus or train or in a car

pasajeros — personas que viajan con el conductor en un autobús, un tren o un auto

For More Information/Más información

Fiction Books/Libros de ficción

Crews, Donald. *School Bus*. New York: Greenwillow Books, 1984.

Hoban, Lillian. *Arthur's Back to School Day*. New York: HarperCollins, 1996.

Nonfiction Books/Libros de no ficción

Klingel, Cynthia and Robert B. Noyed. *School Buses*. Chanhassen, Minn.: Child's World, 2000.

Ready, Dee. *School Bus Drivers*. Mankato, Minn.: Bridgestone Books, 1998.

Web Sites/Páginas Web

The Buses of Sunnydown Garage
www.sunnydownbuses.com
Games and stories about a group of buses

Index/Índice

About the Author/Información sobre la autora

Jacqueline Laks Gorman is a writer and editor. She grew up in New York City and began her career working on encyclopedias and other reference books. Since then, she has worked on many different kinds of books. She lives with her husband and children, Colin and Caitlin, in DeKalb, Illinois.

Jacqueline Laks Gorman es escritora y editora. Creció en Nueva York, y se inició en su profesión editando enciclopedias y otros libros de consulta. Desde entonces ha trabajado en muchos tipos de libros. Vive con su esposo y sus hijos, Colin y Caitlin, en DeKalb, Illinois.